HOW TO OVERCOME SALES OBJECTIONS IN SEO AND LAND THE SALE OF LIFE A TIME!

A Book about Selling SEO for SEO Service Providers

By Ejeke P. C

Excell Marketing Group
https://www.easyimreviews.com/

My Free Gift to You for Buying This Book, Grab The PDF...

https://www.easyimreviews.com/digital-marketing-statistics-pdf/

These are digital marketing stats to help you grow your business fast!

LEGAL DISCLAIMER:

Any earnings or income statements, or earnings or income examples, are only estimates of what we think you could earn. There is no assurance you'll do as well. If you rely upon our figures, you must accept the risk of not doing as well. Where specific income figures are used, and attributed to an individual or business, those persons or businesses have earned that amount. There is no assurance you'll do as well. If you rely upon our figures; you must accept the risk of not doing as well.

Any and all claims or representations, as to income earnings on this web site, are not to be considered as average earnings. There can be no assurance that any prior successes, or past results, as to income earnings, can be used as an indication of your future success or results.

Monetary and income results are based on many factors. We have no way of knowing how well you will do, as we do not know you, your background, your work ethic, or your business skills or practices. Therefore, we do not guarantee or imply that you will win any incentives or prizes that may be offered, get rich, that you will do as well, or make any money at all. There is no assurance you'll do as well. If you rely upon our figures; you must accept the risk of not doing as well.

Internet businesses and earnings derived there from, have unknown risks involved, and are not suitable for everyone. Making decisions based on any information presented in our products, services, or web site, should be done only with the knowledge that you could experience significant losses, or make no money at all.

All products and services by our company are for educational and informational purposes only. Use caution and seek the advice of qualified professionals. Check with your accountant, lawyer or professional advisor, before acting on this or any information.

Users of our products, services and web site are advised to do their own due diligence when it comes to making business decisions and all information, products, and services that have been provided should be independently verified by your own qualified professionals. Our information, products, and services on this web site should be carefully considered and evaluated, before reaching a business decision, on whether to rely on them. All disclosures and disclaimers made herein or on our site, apply equally to any offers, prizes, or incentives, that may be made by our company.

You agree that our company is not responsible for the success or failure of your business decisions relating to any information presented by our company, or our company products or services.

Does overcoming objections on your sales calls have you stressed? Or are you just sick and tired of objections like these? Well, NOT ANYMORE!

INTRODUCTION

Though this book is written with SEOs in mind, any business or company can use the principles and methods laid out here to achieve impressive results.

This is a book about how you as an SEO service provider (any business for that matter) can tackle problems that are associated with a **sale**.

But no matter what the product or who the other person is; the strategies discussed within this book will help you too. You don't have to be an SEO service provider to benefit from the principles and strategies laid out in this book. They are universal.

It's not about being a pro in business or being smart (though they all do help) but it's about your client. The other guy across the table or the guy on the other end of the phone. You will get to understand what stops a potential client from taking action on your services or products.

I will be breaking down the professional tips anyone and I mean anyone can deploy in their business. These will make you or your sales team skilled in closing sales. These are also the same methods that the most powerful sales companies and agencies use to close the toughest of sales.

So, am going to break this down into the following steps. 1st I will present general guidelines on overcoming objections, 2nd, I will move into common client objections followed by a Q&A section then 3rd, the summary of the whole process.

By the end of the book, you will have all you need to overcome the most common objections in SEO and close the sale. This, of course, opens you up to have better conversations with a potential client when you are in the middle of a pitch.

So let's get down to it. But 1st, before we get into "how to overcome sales objections", let's talk a little about the "why" the **reasons objections** happen to start with.

WHY DO SALES OBJECTIONS HAPPEN?

So, why do sales objections happen? Objections happen because a section or a portion of your sales process is weak. You didn't build enough rapport, you didn't ask them enough questions about them, you didn't give them a chance to talk – you talked for 45 minutes to an hour, and you didn't allow them to speak up. I mean, when you do a pitch, it's not a webinar; it's a pitch. And a pitch is only valuable if you're taking half of the time.

Behind every objection is a failure of a salesman to answer the burning question for every prospect, which is "What's in it for me?" SEO is an investment, what do they get in return? And if you don't have a good understanding, if you don't have a strong belief system that supports you, you won't know how to address the objection.

How you address an objection can be the tipping point for a prospect to buy your service or buy it from somebody else. However, with the right approach, you can easily win the conversation, turn that objection into an opportunity, and, ultimately, close that prospect.

Now that we are familiar with why sales objections happen, let's try and answer the question; does selling SEO need to be hard? Keep reading.

WHY SELLING SEO DOESN'T HAVE TO BE HARD

Okay, so selling SEO services isn't that hard, it's a lot easier than you think. As easy as any worthwhile endeavor can be. Most times, people's feelings that SEO is difficult is because of some deep-rooted misconceptions. Let's try and address them.

Misconception 1: I Need to Learn Everything about SEO

Think you need to learn everything about SEO to sell it?

The truth is you can start offering SEO services by understanding some of the core principles.

You should know enough to understand yourself how it works as well as accurately explain it to your client…but you don't need to be an expert at every facet of SEO to get started.

Knowing everything about SEO could result in you shooting yourself in the foot while in conversation with clients. There's no better way to create a glazed look in someone's eyes than talking about SEO in-depth.

Your job isn't to become an SEO expert: It's to translate SEO into a results-focused description that your client can understand.

That way, you can focus on painting the picture of how results through SEO will help their business. Doing that will help you close the deal.

Misconception 2: I Have to Do All the Work In-House

It's understandable to think that you might not have the time or ability to do the actual SEO work.

Here's the beautiful thing about offering these services: You don't have to do it yourself!

You can consistently deliver quality SEO work to your clients by enlisting the help of a white label SEO service, like The SEOResllers of which I am a partner.

In case the term "white labelling" or "reseller SEO" is unfamiliar to you, it refers to work done by another company on your behalf and sold under your name.

In addition to not having to perform SEO work yourself in-house, white labelling allows you to focus on providing great service to your clients by entrusting the work to professional SEO practitioners.

At SEOreseller, we have designed our services for scalability and we work with thousands of agencies around the world.

By using a scalable solution, you can offer SEO services to as many clients as you want without worrying about having to hire and train employees.

Time is your most precious commodity. To offer SEO services while holding on to as much time as you can, focus on managing the client and let us do the work!

Want some help getting started? Just **GO HERE TO SIGN UP** with us and we'll get you all set up!

Ok, now that we have the most common misconceptions out of the way, let's get into what SEO knowledge you need to start selling.

THE SALES PROCESS

Just to put things in perspective for you, overcoming objections is just 1 step in a series of steps that you need in every **Sales Process**. Of course, depending on who you ask, the Sales Process could be up to 8 steps or even 12 steps. For me, I prefer to keep things as simple as possible.

For example, Brian Tracy has a 7 step Sales Process. Steven Tulman of Social Pulse Marketing talked about a 10 step Sales Process in a piece he wrote for Status Magazine.

But the thing is, it doesn't matter how many steps you choose to adopt, there is always some form of objection on each step. Let me briefly run through the 7 Step Sales Process that I like to follow.

Step 1 Prospecting and Initial Contact

Before you start selling online, you have to know who you want to sell to. As simple as that may sound, but believe me when I say lots of people get that wrong including yours truly. When I was starting, I'll just put something up online without a clue who my customer or audience is. The biggest mistake to make.

The question is, how do you get to know them? Simple really. You have what could arguably be one of the greatest inventions of the 20th century, your mobile phone. Combine that with Google and the power of the internet and boom you are in business. Simply Google your customers. It can't get any simpler than that in the 1st step.

Then when you have found them, do the next natural thing, contact them. They won't sell your product to themselves. You have to put yourself in front of them and create that rapport that will carry you till you make the sale.

Get them to like you, trust you, be as close as you can to them without appearing creepy. No one will want to buy anything from you if you come across as creepy. Make them laugh…… Victor Borge said laughter is the shortest distance between 2 people. That gets you the best results trust me. It's difficult for some not to buy if you can make them feel good especially if they need what you have to sell.

After you build rapport, you **qualify** them. You try to figure out if your service is a match for their needs. Because if it's not, don't sell to them, right? There's only one reason you should be selling to someone, and that's because you can genuinely add value to their business, or their goals - you're able to help grow the business.

Step 2 Qualifying

The next in the process is qualifying them. This means; while you are gaining their trust and trying your hardest to make them laugh, you smoothly move into determining if they are a good match for your product or service.

Frankly, there is no need to push to sell someone something they don't need just so you can make a quick buck. What does that say about you and your business? That's the quickest way to sell yourself out of business. You just want to help them get what they want, value. That way they will be more than happy to give you their money in exchange.

The qualifying process involves you or your sales team asking Qualifying questions that are typically related to budget, authority, need and timeline.

Step 3 Needs Assessment

After the qualification is done, then you move to **Needs Assessment.** This is a process of asking follow up questions to understand the prospect. The goal is to thoroughly understand the prospect's situation, challenges, and motivations to potentially make a change by purchasing your product or service. There might be cases that the prospect doesn't quite know what they want or what will help the most in their business.

That's where your sales team will really earn their keep. You or your sales team need to listen more then you speak. Let the prospect empty themselves. It will also help them to anticipate any objects that the client might have.

Some example of questions that you might want to ask are-

What did you like or dislike about your previous provider?
What business problem are you hoping we'll be able to solve?
Describe your current situation.
Tell me how this situation will look when you've addressed your current business problem.

When all questions have been discussed, it is important that your reps verify their understanding of what the prospect told them. The best way for them to do this is by recapping what they heard and requesting confirmation. This ensures that the rep is on the same page as the prospect before proceeding to the next step. If needed, additional questions may be asked to clear up any areas the rep misinterpreted.

Step 4 Sales Pitch or Product Demo

In this sales stage, you can now tie the value of your product, service, or solution to your client's needs, challenges, and desired end state. To do this, you have to clearly communicate the corresponding features and benefits of your product offering.

You will agree with me this is a very good reason why you or your sales team should have a clear understanding of what is discussed during the need's assessment stage. This is critical if you hope to have a quality pitch and demo depending on what your products or services are.

Be sure that your reps make note of any specific benefits in which the prospect is most enthusiastic about. At the end of this stage, a proposal, if appropriate to your product or service, is typically scheduled for a mutually agreed upon date.

Step 5 Proposal and Handling Objections

You know, not all products and services require a separate proposal. Like I said above, depending on what you have, you might want to adapt it to suit your client's needs and aspirations. This should be done in such a way that all the information you have gathered so far since you started communicating with your client, are put into consideration and addressed properly.

It doesn't make much sense if the client has told you all their problems and you can't demonstrate a way that your services or products help solve them.

Try to focus or at the very least put a bit more emphasis on those areas that you discover are your prospect's biggest concern. It's at this stage that you **experience objections and concerns** which is the main topic of this book, *how to overcome sales objections and land the sale of a lifetime*. I will get to that soon enough, but just to close off the 7 steps in sales; here are the remaining two steps. It is just two more steps in what may be a very long sales cycle.

While this may seem to be one of the most important steps in the whole process, and in many ways, it is, but you won't get to this stage if you do not do a good job in all the previous 5 steps.

Step 6 The Close.

This is the point where your prospect commits to purchase or sign on to your product or service. Either they do this or they don't at this stage. There are hundreds of different closing techniques, tips, and tricks, but the most important thing to remember is that it is not a standalone event.

When the sale is made, prospects agree on your terms and price or negotiate for mutually beneficial ones. All objections have been addressed and all details are finalized for delivery, fulfilment, or related actions. This may also involve introductions to others in your company who will be handling these next steps.

Step 7 Following Up

This means exactly what it says, follow up with your client to make sure everything is good. This also may include, asking for more or expansion of the service you are already offering and as well as asking for referrals.

A great way to continue these relationships is through marketing communications such as updates about new offerings, industry news, an e-newsletter, or some sort of interactive rewards program. This way, your customers will always think of your company first when they have a related requirement or a friend who has one.

So, okay back to closing. As I said, you won't get to step 6 not to talk of step 7 if you don't carry out the 1st 5 steps properly and in order. Then and only then can you have **a flawless close.**

Now, the flawless close can't be done when objections happen, because most of the time there was a weakness at some point in your sales process. Either you didn't get them to laugh, you didn't get them to trust you, you didn't get them to like you at some point in the conversation. Or you didn't listen to them during the qualifying phase, or you may not have matched the right product to the right need. There are several reasons why, and we'll go through some of those reasons now.

So, we get into the main discussion of sales in SEO proper. Later on, I will be talking about some typical industry questions that you probably will likely encounter in the industry. They are classic questions and answers that lots of SEO service providers are asked all the time. One, in particular, is about the value of SEO.

You see, a lot of business owners know about their business and probably have and maintain a web presence. But they struggle to make the connection between their business and how SEO on their web property will translate into sales and profit.

COMMON OBJECTIONS

Pricing is one of the most common objections because there are lots of cheap services online. The issues are that many of the online services often stack up deliverables that don't bring significant results. You can rebut these statements by looking at the other offer and clearly explaining how much more value you will bring.

Another common objection is asking for a **one-off or a trial**. Here you can explain that Google wants to see consistency in your site becoming an authority as opposed to quick pops. Additionally, Google wants to see a holistic strategy including on Page optimization, links, and content.

But let me take them one after another and go drill deeper.

1- The Value of SEO

In discussing *the value of SEO*, when you talk to clients there are usually two scenarios. One is that they don't really get it. I mean how does what you do for them in terms of SEO translates into sales? Bear in mind that they don't see the results right away. Of course, SEO takes a while to kick in but even then, they won't really understand it unless you show them the starts and then walk them through how that is as a result of what you did a couple of weeks back. The second one is that you probably failed to listen to your prospect.

So, let's take them one after the other.

The 1st one-

Yes, sometimes your client won't get it so you have to educate them on that. Other times, it could be that you are not talking to the right person in the company or business. I mean the person whose job it is to make decisions within the company; you are basically talking to the gatekeeper. So, what you want to here is to be able to leverage some SEO stats - you have to know your stats off the bat.

So, later on in the book, I will be providing you with some pointers on what you should say in terms of stats. This shouldn't be a surprise. If you did a Google search, you will find that over 90% of sites on the internet are operated by small and medium-sized businesses. Out of this at least %91, you have about 80% to 90% of the folks behind these sites don't know much about SEO and it impacts their business.

So, that tells you that education is key here. And if you are going to do well as an SEO service provider, then you should make education a major focus in your business. It's not just your education, as the rules change often but also the education of your prospects.

Education is part of the game. You have a time frame within which you are meant to get that sale. You need to create desire, build excitement, and help your client see the value in the service that you are providing. You have to let them see just how much better their business will be doing and that it's capable of growing beyond what they can imagine.

So, SEO is an education game; you have to assume that everyone you talk to, it will be rare and few and far between that they will have knowledge that's equal to or better than yours. You will educate most of the people that you talk to about SEO.

And that leverages trust on your end. If you have enough SEO stats or digital marketing stats to throw out there, that just tells your client you know your industry and that you know what is going on right now.

The 2nd one-

It says you failed to listen to your prospect; this goes back to what I just mentioned earlier about you going through your sales process. Now remember it's not linear; you have to make sure that you build desire, you have to make sure that you offer value, and if you fail to do one of those, at your sales steps or your sales process, then you are probably missing out on the opportunity of closing the sale.

Now, as I told you before, I have made similar mistakes in the past. I have had a time where I have gone off the rails myself. I had this opportunity to pitch for an eCommerce site. But essentially, it became a pitch where they kept on talking about rankings and traffic, rankings and traffic, rankings and traffic... and repeatedly, the customer had said, what I want is s functioning site with traffic that wants to buy stuff.

Underneath all that, what he is really saying is "don't tell me about those technical mumbo-jumbos, just tell me if your skills can solve my problems and show me how". It's that simple.

And as soon as I gave him a yes, he said let's do it and he signed. How simpler can that get? I mean you have to be able to read your prospect in some way or form. Gauge his appetite for risk or his ability to stay with technical stuff.

Now, I'm not devaluing the technical portion of that conversation, because it did prove expertise, meaning he knew without a doubt that we were the pros and that we had their best intentions in mind, and that he saw our moral imperative. But there's only one thing that the business owner needed to hear: "Will doing SEO help me sell my products?"

That's it, that's all he needed to hear. Now, again, while we don't guarantee results, SEOs are experienced enough to make commitments. So, after we signed up to the SEO service, before their sixth month he is pulling in quite a good amount of traffic. But, it's also good to note that there are different kinds of traffic. Just because a site is pulling in tones of traffic that doesn't mean a thing if no one is buying whatever you want to sell. You need to be a bale to bring in buyer traffic. People who have their credit cards in hand and are ready to buy.

And this is an example of listening well to your customers; you have to ask them questions, they have to be talking half the time through the pitch because they don't want to hear "I'll rank you" and they don't want to hear "I'll get you a thousand visitors a day". They want to sell their products, that's the business goal. Your job as a salesman is to marry that business goal to what your service can deliver.

- *Pro Tips 1*

Below are just some of the stats that you need to pay attention to, and I think these are some of the most important stats for you to know.

- **93% of buying experiences begin on search**. Not being present on search translates to lost opportunities for the client, so if you're ever thinking of just going for traditional marketing, think again.
- Can drive up to **x22 ROI** per dollar spent, and
- There are **60 billion** websites online today (and growing); can you believe that? 60 billion websites.
- **91%** of those aren't optimized. That's a sad story, but good news for SEOs out there.
- SEO is a **16-billion-dollar** industry, so, you know, if I were you, l will be trying my best to get into the industry right now.

Now, let me just translate the opportunity for you. What that means is if only 10% of websites are optimized, SEO can easily be larger by a factor of 10. It could easily be a **160-billion-dollar** industry; it's not a saturated industry, it's a very green field.

- *Pro Tip 2*

Translate the value of SEO into terms a decision-maker can understand. This is what I talked about earlier, about making sure that your client understands the value of SEO, and make sure that you don't overwhelm him with SEO jargon, just being able to show value to them is important. Having stats on top of your head or off the bat establishes trust signals.

Now, I'll move on to the next.

1- Pricing

This is a meaty conversation, and I had some, you know, not bad experiences, but challenging experiences on this one. So, I will be talking about pricing, and this is one of the most common objections I get, and you probably get as well from your clients. A lot of your partners would say, that the clients find the pricing expensive. Or you might tell me, or tell your project managers, "I find your pricing expensive." And, if you're reading between the lines, the translation of this objection is "*I do not see the value of what you just offered me, what you just pitched me.*"

That is exactly the problem. If you have a customer with a problem, an itch to be precise. He wants that itch scratched and you are not doing that. Then you are of no help or value to him. If a client says that your price is expensive then you haven't shown them that you can help them scratch the itch. If they know you can, the price will take second stage right away.

So, this goes back to the sales process of building desire or offering value to what you're providing. But really, our pricing isn't more expensive, and what I always like to tell the partners that I talk to is that we never claim that we're the cheapest. That's one, and I always go into probing when I get these kinds of objections. I ask them, do you really get results for what you pay for? And, you know, you have to make sure that these clients are actually getting the right results, the right type of reporting, and we do provide that.

Working with my **partners and sign up**, we can offer your clients results, we offer you client dashboard logins, so your clients can access the google analytics dashboard in real-time and view the performance of your site and our SEO services. We provide real-time reporting that comes at the of every cycle, we have the executive summary reports, and we have white papers and marketing guides.

So, I love this objection. This is the objection that is probably, for me the easiest one to overcome. Clients find the pricing expensive; so, my primary strategy really, is to tell people.

**A} we're not the cheapest provider and
B} you get what you pay for.**

Which really is the easiest thing to pitch off the top of your head. Now, let me give you a couple of reasons why this is easy.

You might not be aware, but it's actually normal, you can have end clients. You probably could have customers that come to you directly, especially locally. And despite facing the same objections that so many others face, you could be closing 8 out of 10 for every pitch. So, that will translate to an 80% close rate.

And you can overcome this because in order to make sure that you aren't cannibalizing potential profits with your partner agencies, (if you have those) you also have double or triple your prices locally. Now, why is it so easy to overcome?

First of all, I'll go back to sales. It's a belief system; I've seen how effective the service is, I've seen the businesses that it's grown, and I personally sincerely believe, that when we work on a campaign, they're going to get their money's worth, and I'm doing them a favor by closing to the best of my ability because they want to grow the same way that other successful businesses have grown.

So, by having a strong belief system in the service that you provide, you do not shy away from a pricing objection. So, I'll give you a great example though, when you cave to a pricing objection. Imagine that you take on a client who has been to **another agency**. (https://www.whitebasemedia.com/) And you take a look at their site and find that

2- He was being charged say $300 for SEO

3- You find no optimization done on the site
4- non-existent or weak links from free blogs
5- a tone of blog comments (doesn't work today by the way)

And the entire site is missing lots of the most important things that actually work today.
1- No quality signals to Google,
2- No trust signals,
3- no well-crafted digital footprint,
4- No authority sculpting inside the website, nothing.
5- No rich snippets inside the web page.

In his mind, this other SEO guy, he thinks he is saving money by only spending $300 at cost on his SEO. But in reality, he lost some of the relationships along the way; relationships he will never be able to get back. And if for example, he has 11 other clients that he had onboarded, he personally spent out of pocket $300 for each of those accounts. What's 12 x $300? He was spending over $3,600 every month at cost, and he was burning relationships while doing that.

At the end of a year and a half, which is 18 months, he would have poured $64,800 down the drain. For nothing. Right? So really, you get what you pay for, and this is why I strongly advise that you need to be very selective with the **partners** you take in. So, for any client, you take on you need to be careful and make sure you can deliver on any promise that you make. And why is that? You don't want to destroy relationships; you want repeat business and even better will be a referral and more business. Who doesn't like that?

And you have to have a great belief system about your service. Because the client doesn't know that you're good, and if you are not convinced of your expertise then you won't convince them either

- *Pro Tips 1*

No worries. So, on the pro tips, don't dance around the pricing objection, address it. I mean, sure you can dance while you talk to your client over the phone, but don't dance around the pricing objection, address it. I'm not saying you have to affirm it, but you have to address it. Acknowledge the objection, then isolate the objection and act on it.

There are three golden rules in pricing, and I will talk about **Primacy** and **Recency** in a bit, but let me just go through the 1, 2, and 3 Golden Rules.

1- **You never mention pricing first**, and
2- **You never let it stand alone.** Lastly,
3- **Never mention pricing last**.

Having been on the internet and doing marketing, I have come to identify these 3 golden rules. These three golden rules will help you to overcome the pricing objection, or preventing it from becoming an objection.

Rule #1- is that you never mention pricing first; there is a phenomenon called Primacy. The first thing we hear tends to be stickier than everything else in the middle.

So how do you practice this? You don't go into a pitch, and start with "Hi, today I'm offering you a $2,000 package that will do this, this, this..." It doesn't work. The moment you say $2,000, you might as well sing and dance and blah your way through the conversation. They will not hear anything past $2,000. So, you never mention it first.

Rule #2- Next, you never let it stand alone. So, you don't say, you don't go through the pitch, whether at the first or at the last, and tell them "And you get all this service, and look forward to these results, at the end of six months, all of that only for a six-month investment of $12,000."

What do you think? So, you never let it stand alone. You never let the pricing stand-alone. It's always... you always have to sandwich it between details. You will need to tell them, "The service plus this, this, this, and for that price, and for that investment, you get this, this, this, this." And you never mention it first, right?

Rule #3- Now, never mentioning pricing last. If there is anything more powerful than the concept of Primacy, it's the concept of Recency. And that is, the brain is biased to retain the last thing that was said. This is so powerful, that whenever you call a help desk, or a credit card line, or whatnot, they'll tell you the brand first, so that they leverage Primacy, and they'll tell you their name last. So that you remember the name of the person you talked to.

The brain is biased to treat the last information or the last thing it heard to be the most important. When you say "And you get all of this for a six-month contract price of $12,000", everything you just said, you might as well erase. So that's the concept of Primacy, never letting it stand alone, and Recency.

- *Pro-tip 2*

If you don't work alone and you have partners that you attach yourself to, then it's important that you mark-up service by more than x1. I have to urge you, and actually, recommend that you mark-up services by x2 or even x2.5 retail cost when your portfolio is already built.

And actually, this next pro tip is a partner of a fellow SEO service provider. In the UAE because that's his market, he gives 30% on their first 90 days.

Right, so they've got a **partner** in the Middle East, and the strategy that he does to get people into contracts {because he does sell them contracts, not a prepaid subscription basis}, and his strategy is, he only doubles the pricing that they have on the dashboard during the first 90 days of the contract. And then, he proves that he can deliver results.

Now, in SEO the advantage is well, he is in a very ripe market, the Middle East is probably virginal to SEO - almost no one does it there, no matter how sophisticated and how advanced they already are. So almost any website he touches and implements On Page on almost overnight turns to gold. They're so convinced at the value that he's very successful at converting them from 3-month contracts to 6-month contracts. And by the time they cross the 3rd-month threshold, he puts them on regular pricing, which is the standard x3 of what my friend's services are.

And this is a good way to approach it strategically.

1- No Guarantees

Alright, let's move on to our next sales objection: no guarantees. This is one of my favorites, actually, and I sometimes get a laugh at this because a lot of our people still have these kinds of issues. I can't get approval for a service that has no committed results. Now sometimes that would come from a **partner** or their client. And really, the question there is; why don't you guarantee rankings? It really comes from them.

If I could just steer the question a bit, why do we look for guarantees, right? Why do people find guarantees attractive? We all look for guarantees because there is a concept called buyer's remorse, and buyer's remorse is very powerful. It's three times more powerful than desire. So, to steer away from buyer's remorse, everyone is looking for that warranty, that guarantee, that "30 day" return policy or something of that sort.

But you can't do that with SEO, and I'll explain why.

It's very simple, because for example, if you get to talk to someone over the phone, maybe another vendor telling you "I can guarantee first page rankings on your website in the next 30 days."

And I hear this too! I hear this every week, every time the phone rings a few customers will say "My previous provider promised me position 1. My previous provider promised me this. My freelancer said he could get me on Page 1 in X months."

Exactly, and you know what, I always tell them, and this comes from the bottom of my heart, drop the phone whenever you hear someone say that. Or you, just change your phone number, get a new sim card, and destroy your landline phone, whatever. Don't ever talk to that partner again.

Exactly, because at the end of the day, if you're talking about SEO, there's no one really who can guarantee rankings. There are only two ways for you to be able to do that; the first one is you're probably directly in control of the algorithm, meaning you're working for Google. And that's impossible because not a lot of people do that. And not even Larry Page manipulates rankings.

The second one is, they're probably doing some Black Hat SEO, which is something you want to stay away from.

So, I'll dive in a bit deeper into that. What controls the organic rankings is a very complex, very intelligent, and very expensive algorithm. And no one controls that, not even Google engineers control how powerful their portion of the algorithm is. The algorithm determines the page that's best for the user based on the query that they do. Google's core is search, so they always want to give you the results that matter the most - the ones that matter to the users.

Barring you being able to control - now while no one can control the algorithm, which means you can't place someone deliberately on position 1 - you can manipulate it. You can game it. And gaming the algorithm is dangerous because you'll benefit from it in the short term, but you don't benefit from it in the long term. So, anybody that promises you position 1 rankings can only really do that by doing two things: either gain control of the full Google algorithm or manipulate the algorithm in a Black Hat way. And that's why you want to stay away from it.

Also, sometimes we get asked, "Why don't you guys guarantee traffic?" It's the same method or same approach that we take, we can't guarantee traffic. But, here's the big but, SEOs or Project Managers actually, they're all **partnered up with seasoned SEO experts.** (https://www.easyimreviews.com/blog/seo-reseller-review-best-seo-reseller-program/) And they're pretty much experienced enough to set soft goals on what their clients can expect in terms of the traffic you will get on an SEO campaign.

Now, Storytime, before we go to the pro tips. This story is from my **friends and partners**. And this is what I mean when I say soft goals. One of the clients that they had was an airliner, and the airliner's goal was to gain a million more in traffic through that year by investing in SEO. They took a look at the site, they realized that there was a lot of opportunities, a lot of low hanging fruit. They didn't have, they didn't optimize for any keywords that said "flights from A to B".

And there are so many variations of that keyword they can create because the airline flew so many places. And by optimizing for those, they wound up not adding one million, but almost three million in traffic to them. So, what that means is they took on the business, even though what they wanted was a million more traffic. But given where they stood, the **SEO** was experienced enough to know "Yeah, I can do a million traffic. Against a website like this, with that many low hanging fruits? I can get a million traffic on to the site."

The other one that they worked on that worked off of something similar is a bank that had three million in monthly traffic. And they wanted to increase that by a million every month. And when my partners saw that there was also a lot of low hanging fruit, meaning they had *hundreds* of pages that were not being crawled by the search engine, that were not getting indexed therefore not ranking opportunity... when they saw that, they realized that they could get a million in traffic easy. And that's why they said yes, and six months in, they got three million more in traffic every month.

Alright, on to our pro tips for no guarantees.

- **Pro Tips 1**

First, no one knows what you are selling. Be able to leverage expertise, know your stats, and you won't have to go through that conversation about guarantees anymore. And our methodology works 80% of the time, ranks 60% of the keywords in the first six months. I've asked this same question to a couple of **partners** that I have talked to, and this is very true. Any SEO strategist that is worth his salt will tell you the same thing.

So, last but not the least,

- **Pro Tip 2**

Talk to your project manager about soft goals. If you don't have **a project manager or partners yet then go here and sign up pronto**.

Yup! Okay, now so go do that.

1- Bad Experience with Previous Agencies

I've been burned by bad SEO providers before I started. So, let's take something back from the Plato Playbook: "How you see the problem is the problem." Right? If this objection had a subtitle, the subtitle would read "I understand the value of SEO, but I want a provider that I can trust."

Now, this is not such a problem for you, as it isn't for one of our **powerhouse partners**. (https://www.easyimreviews.com/blog/seo-reseller-review-best-seo-reseller-program/) One of their powerhouse partners actually looks for people that have been burned by bad SEO providers before. Because in his mind, it doesn't translate as "ooh, problem". In his mind, it translates into "hmm, qualified."

Why? Because they've worked with SEOs before, they know

what to expect, they know how important optimization is, and so on. They no longer have to sell the service. They just have to sell themselves. So, the only thing they work on in the sales process is the rapport portion of the sales process. Now, one of the things I've come to experience is that I would literally lose sleep when campaigns don't rank.

I like ranking everything I touch; I like turning them to gold. I have lost clients just as my friends and other SEOs have. And some partners have taken campaigns away from them, to test another provider, only to bring them back two, three, four months in, with a manual penalty inside the search console.

And personally, and I don't want to sound dramatic, but for me, that's a heart-breaking experience. Because we would have worked on that campaign for three, four, five, six months... and all the work has gone down the drain, and now we have to be the ones to recover whatever the cheap provider had done to get results for the website.

It's difficult for folks to understand that a website puts food on someone's table. So I always tell my clients when you work with us or **my partners directly**, I think what you'll need to know is that we understand that your website and your customer's website, they put food on your table. We take that very seriously. And you as an SEO expert should take that seriously if you want to keep putting food on the table for you and your family.

But now, going back to the concept of getting burned by bad SEO providers... they're out there. They can be closed. Given that one of our largest providers specifically leverages people that have been burned by bad SEO providers. You know, all he has to do is work on his likeability. And then he lets the **methodology** do the rest.

- *Pro Tips 1*

Now, let's move on to a pro tip. You have to leverage expertise and trust signals to differentiate yourself from previous providers. If you're not new at this game, bring your testimonials. We've even had partners that said, "Can I talk to one, two, three of your clients? From the U.S., from three different regions, because I want to hear what experience with you is like."

And you know, of course, they speak up for us, because we help them grow their business. But you have to be able to leverage that. Now, let's say you've been in the game for a while, and here is one of the most difficult objections to overcome: "My previous SEO provider has gotten me penalized before, how do I know you're not going to do that?"

And there are three ways to respond specifically to that variation of this objection. The first way to respond would be "Nope, none of my clients have been penalized", especially if you're new, none of your clients would have been penalized. The next one is if you have had the experience of working with bad providers before; that did get your clients in trouble, the question is: did you take responsibility for what happened?

If the answer is yes, then you can tell them "Yes, and here's what we did to recover them at our expense." Now, if you've been in the game and never had a client penalized, the best way to respond to this is "Yes, we've worked with clients that have penalties from previous providers, but we have a 100% batting average at removing penalties."

Because it's true, our partners (https://www.easyimreviews.com/blog/seo-reseller-review-best-seo-reseller-program/) have a 100% average at removing penalties. And their methodology is the methodology you can adapt to your own business. Therefore, if they bat at 100%, then so do you.

There, now a bit of caution: there's a wrong way to approach this specific objection and all its different variations. When they say that they have been burned by bad providers before, I think a lot of salespeople find it all too easy to say "Oh, who is your previous provider? Yeah, they're evil, they're the spawn of Satan."

You don't want to badmouth the previous provider. In the same way, like in the rule of an interview, you don't want to hire an employee that all they do in the interview is badmouth their previous employer, you don't badmouth a previous provider. And then the next one is you don't put clients in a negative mindset, partially by badmouthing the provider. If you guys get stuck on the badmouth of the previous provider, you're making your close less likely because you're putting your client in a negative frame of mind.

And in sales, there is a concept called putting your client in a Yes frame of mind. That's a different topic altogether. So, I'll move us on to the next one.

1- Keyword and Search Volume Limits

So, this is to me, more than an objection. It's really more of something you need to understand better. Keyword and search volume limits; why do you have a limit to the number of keywords and search volume? I get asked about this almost all the time, and this is where we get a little bit technical because some SEO campaigns are more difficult than others and require more work.

If you check my **partner's dashboard store** and you view all the details in their Local SEO or Organic SEO packages, you'll see that there are different tiers in their packages. They have keyword and search volume limits to reflect this. Again, I will say this: they can rank 60% of keywords on the first page, in the next six months, because the limits are there.

And some competitors will just claim the credit for incidental rankings. In our company and **our partners,** we provide you executive summary reports every month, so you'll see the target keywords we have, how much of them have ranked up, how much have trended up, but there are also keywords there that we would show you that happen to be like bonus keywords or incidental rankings. We don't claim that we did that for you guys, we just present it to you guys so that you can offer more value to the client.

Right, now I'll just reinforce what I just said. Some campaigns are more difficult than others; working on a keyword "**lawyer in Oregon**", or in any city in Oregon for that matter, is significantly easier than working on just the keyword "**lawyer**" - incidentally, the most difficult one is "Houston".

And so, there's really no way to measure which one is more competitive and which one is not, and you can't use the competitiveness metric inside AdWords because AdWords is PPC. The competitiveness metric there is a PPC metric and not an organic metric. The only true organic metric is the number of times a query is executed for your client.

Therefore, **we and our partners** use the search volume to indicate the level of ease or difficulty of winning a keyword. Now, going to competitor's claiming credit for incidental rankings. I have seen SEO providers, retail and wholesale like our **partners**, people who provide **white-label services like our partners**, wherein their report they say "Oh we ranked all these keywords." You know, for 250 dollars, we ranked you for 50 keywords.

Now, we don't do that. But it is true when you work on one keyword, it's like iron filings to a magnet, they all move together. But we don't claim that we did that, we only claim credit for keywords that we worked on, and if there are incidental rankings, we report it, meaning we tell them "Oh, and our work, by the way, had the incidental benefit for these terms too." But we don't take credit for work we don't do.

Let's move on to the pro tips for this one.

- *Pro Tips 1*

The first one is that getting this objection indicates that you're on the right track. You're not talking about pricing, you're not talking about any value-adding proposition, and this one is about getting technical on a service. If you're talking about this objection already, you're on the right path. It's a sign that you've piqued their interest because their questions have started to level up, and objections like this are opportunities to educate your clients and demonstrate your expertise.

So, the next objection.

1- Client Has an Existing Provider

The client has an existing provider. Oh my, this is a meaty one.

Now, out of all these objections so far, I think this is the only really difficult one.

I already have an existing solution, why should I switch to you? There are different variations of this objection.

- I already have a freelancer doing my work, that's one.
- Second is I'm comfortable with my current provider, I don't feel the need to switch.

But what you are hearing, if you read between the lines is the client is just averse to change.

They're happy with the current provider. They're still getting not good results; you have to understand that behind every loyal client is an awesome salesman.

So, let me just zoom us out for a bit. Remember that when you're looking for your opportunities when you're prospecting for leads when you're prospecting for customers. You don't try to target customers in positions 1, 2, and 3. In fact, you don't target or you don't prospect leads from the first page. You prospect them from the second page, from the third page, to however else lower down the road.

But you don't try to win a pitch - especially if you're new, don't try to win a pitch for someone that's already ranking for their keywords on the first page. Do your research. Make sure that you are talking to someone who you can help significantly. Now, if you're talking to someone, a website owner who has a website that is only ranking on the third page, for a term that's obviously relevant to them, you have an opportunity.

And yet they're averse to change. They don't want to switch providers. What that should tell you is these guys have an awesome salesman. So, how do you overcome this objection? You overcome this objection by getting them to become really uncomfortable with their results.

- **Pro Tips 1**

So, "I already have a freelancer doing my work." Leverage the premium experience you can offer with the technology at your **agency's dashboard.** (https://www.easyimreviews.com/blog/seo-reseller-review-best-seo-reseller-program/) Show them the dashboard, freelancers don't have dashboards. They have Google Docs, and they have Excel Sheets.

"I'm comfortable with my current provider, I don't feel the need to switch." Well if you're comfortable with your current provider buddy, are you comfortable being on the second page?

So, this is how you do it - don't badmouth them! Don't badmouth the current provider. But do get them uncomfortable with the fact that they're on the second page, that gets at best 24% click-through throughout the page and the third page which at best gets %13 click through throughout the page.

Now don't try to pitch clients that are already in top spots, find your opportunities on the second and third pages. But if they're comfortable with their provider and they're on the second or third page, they're just telling you that they love their salesman. You got to be the more lovable salesman.

HOW TO OVERCOME THE OBJECTIONS

We've discussed the sales objections and their solutions. But generally, here is what you should know and can do across the board.

So, general guidelines to overcoming an objection. Step 1 is to acknowledge the objection.

Step 1- Acknowledge

When potential clients raise a sales objection, the biggest mistake you can do is ignore it. Always acknowledge the objection. This shows that you're recognizing their concern and listening to what they're saying, which is why you should start with the phrase "I hear you/I understand." However, there's a difference between acknowledgment and affirmation. When you acknowledge an objection, it doesn't mean that you're agreeing with them.

Step 2- Isolate

It's important to nail down the main concern of your prospect. Don't let it sprout two or three more issues. You don't want them to tell you that your pricing is too high, the value isn't clear to their business, and the service is too complicated for them. You need to figure out the sole reason behind their objection. This is where you start asking probing questions.

Step 3- Own

This is where you take accountability to address their concerns. Don't leave an objection hanging without your commitment. Taking ownership is a way of gaining the trust of your prospect. Instead of saying, "Let me check with the team how to go about this," say, "I'll dive right into this and get back to you by {insert time and day}."

Step 4- Act

Nothing gets done if you don't follow through with your commitment. Once you've determined the reason behind their objection, act on it. Don't promise the moon and deliver anything less because if you do, you're going to lose the trust of your prospect.

Use Special Offers to Help Them Cross the Finish Line

You can use special offers to push them off the fence. It's handy to always have something to give them on top of what you've listed.

To avoid burning their customers out with too many discounts, **my partners** (https://www.easyimreviews.com/blog/seo-reseller-review-best-seo-reseller-program/) rotate deals on different products every month that they promote through email, ads, and a feature page on our site.

SUMMARY

Alright, so let's summarize everything we have discussed so far. So, in summary,

The first one is the Value of SEO.
I have digital marketing starts for you to download. Go Here to Get It
(https://www.easyimreviews.com/blog/digital-marketing-statistics-infographics/)
- Know your SEO stats.
- Translate the value of SEO into terms a decision-maker can understand.

Next is pricing. Don't dance around the pricing, address it.
Now rules to pricing-
- Don't mention it first,
- Don't let it stand alone,
- Don't mention it last.

On the third one, no guarantees.
- Know what you're selling,
- No one can guarantee rankings and traffic. So be careful who you talk to.
- Most of all just know what you're selling, and know your SEO stats.

Bad experience with previous agencies.
That's not a problem, that's an opportunity. Leverage your expertise, provide trust signals, and sell yourself. The best way to overcome people that have a need for SEO, but won't want to work with an SEO agency, is to prove to them that you're someone with a strong moral imperative to see them succeed.

And on keyword and search volumes.

Objections like these are opportunities to educate the clients and demonstrate your expertise. This; really is telling you that you're on the right path, how you see the problem is the problem, like what Plato said. And really, this is for you to make sure that the client is engaging, thoroughly, and throughout your conversation.

And the client has an existing provider.
- Leverage your premium experience.
- Leverage the technology, and
- Make them uncomfortable with their current results. They're on page 2, right? What's even worse is, if you type their domain name in the generic format of the query and they're not number 1 for their own name, their provider isn't providing a lot of value.

So, if they've got an existing provider, the two things you need to keep in mind are
1- The results are not there, and
2- There's a powerful salesman behind it.

And those are really what you have to overcome. Make them uncomfortable with the results, and leverage a better experience with you.

So, this is what I've been talking about earlier.

ENSURING SATISFACTION AFTER FULFILMENT

In the business of SEO, ensuring client satisfaction after fulfilment is crucial. That's why we made sure you knew how to set the right expectations beforehand.

That being said, unsatisfied customers are bound to happen in any industry. Your reputation for doing good SEO work is more important than keeping money from an individual customer who wasn't satisfied.

Offer great support every step of the way, including after fulfilment, by being available for them. If they express dissatisfaction, make sure their expectations are still realistic and try to correct them if not.

The reality is that every client will eventually cancel, and it's not always your fault. By setting expectations, over-delivering in value, communicating thoroughly, delivering on your service, and asking for feedback, you set yourself up for success.

FOR OUR PARTNERS

So here is, digital marketing stat sheet infographic. (https://www.easyimreviews.com/blog/digital-marketing-statistics-infographics/) These are the changes in the digital marketing landscape, to prompt every business into action. So, we compiled all the latest data from 2016 to guide you through these changes. So if you have access to **our partner's dashboard** (https://www.easyimreviews.com/blog/seo-reseller-review-best-seo-reseller-program/0)already, then this infographic is free for you for signing up with our partners.

Right, and I mean kudos to you for sticking with me to this point. That tells me that you are serious about upping your game in SEO.

Awesome! Alright, so let's move on to our Q&A.

Q&A

I do have a couple of questions here that SEOs are dealing with constantly. So, am going to be addressing this based on the experience I have had working with our partners.

Question #1:
We get clients that have websites that are not web responsive and designed in tables. Is there a workaround for it?
Answer:
Absolutely! Build a new site.

So, on WhiteBaseMedia.Com, if you go there and take a look, you will see that we rebuild websites on WordPress for $1,297 with a two-week turnaround period. So, when we get stuff like this it's always better to just start from scratch. It saves you a lot of time and energy. Think about it, what can you do with that, where would you start from? The best thing to do in this circumstance is to just start from scratch and rebuild it from the ground up.

Also, if you don't redesign the site to modern technological standards, the quality metrics in the algorithm don't work in your favor. So, you want to do them a favor and close them to the best of your ability, and help them build a new site.

Question #2:
Do you have any tips on how to respond to the familiar response from a prospect, "I will think about it"?
Answer:
What could turn the conversation around? Now, what we usually say when we get these kinds of responses from a partner who has just signed up with us, is you know I say I hear you, and I understand where you're coming from, but I would always do the ABC. And that's not Always Be Closing, that's ABC meaning **Always Book your next Call.** (https://www.easyimreviews.com/

blog/seo-reseller-review-best-seo-reseller-program/)

Ask for the available time next week, you know, we'll try to adjust our schedule of course, and see when he or she is available and follow through. Maybe you missed something in the sales process that made him or her think twice.

For us, what we try to leverage in this specific situation is a concept called "ownership". And the company that executes this well is Rolex. The most famous ad by Rolex is the one about Mt. Everest, where they said, "At the top of your Everest, your Rolex waits." Meaning they're transferring the ownership to you already.

And that's what we try to do, we try to get them to give us a URL. So they tell us "I'll think about it". We'll tell them, "That's fine, but while you take your time thinking about it, give me a URL. I'll do an audit for you so that you can see how good we are. That way, you're making a better-informed decision."

Most of the time, when we get the URL, we will almost 100% of the time get the business. Because we will create an awesome audit for them. And it's commitment-free! So that's the best part about it, the fact that there's no commitment involved, the moment that we get the URL we get to work on that URL.

Question #3
How do I respond to a client who sees a penalty within one to two months while I am doing SEO for their website?
Answer:
Wow, now this one is tough, but you can handle it quite nicely. SEO is momentum-driven. A penalty can appear anywhere between, you know, two months later down the road, three months later down the road, coming from a previous SEO agency. If they're seeing the penalty appear, it's usually easy to find out if it's you or if it's the previous provider.

Like take for example if you work with us, we submit every link we create to you. When Google sends you the warning, take for an example it's a partial match penalty, meaning it found a link that it thought was bought or contrived, and it tells the site owner you don't need to do anything.

But we are investigating the nature of this link and if you had anything to do with acquiring it. Google will give you the sample URL that's triggering the penalty, and so all you have to do is match the fact that you have a previous work report from your previous provider? Because this website is not on anything that we tried to acquire for you.

So, it's easy for you to prove that it isn't you. But also, the best thing to do is, the penalty is already there, and your job is to be their advocate. So aside from you proving that it wasn't you, and you do that by just being transparent, you have to be the one that helps them get over the penalty and get their sites appearing on the first page again.

Question #4
Is it wise to customize a package if a client has a low budget just so they can afford your service?
Answer:
Yeah, you can actually do that, you can definitely customize your package if it's necessary for the client, especially if they are on a limited budget.

I can tell you this though, if your clients or if you think or you're in a mindset that small businesses cannot afford the service that might not be entirely true, at least not for every single one of them. We're doing SEO for lawnmowers. We do SEO for dog shops or barbershops; we do all those for them. And if they can afford it, I think your clients can too.

Now, in your experience what do prospects value the most when deciding to buy a product or service? The number one result or the number one answer would result. That would be the number one answer, and that's what everybody will tell you they want, but in our experience, it seems like the largest influencing factor in terms of whether people decide to buy seems to be the salesman.

Like how much they thought the sales man's moral imperative was to see their website grow, or if that agency took a personal stake in seeing their business grow. But it seems to be more the relationship factor than it is the results. The results matter, or else you know, then we would spend $20,000 a month figuring out how to build better relationships than spending $20,000 every month figuring out how to do a better service. But we do spend it on the service, because of the results matter.

But in our experience, the strongest turning point for close rate is the likeability of the salesman.

Question #5

Can you help me to train my sales staff to be able to respond to these objections?"

Answer:

My answer would be an all caps, absolutely YES. When you **opt-in with our partners,** (https://www.easyimreviews.com/blog/seo-reseller-review-best-seo-reseller-program/) you have access to your dashboard, and when you sign up for the first time, there's a kick start call link right there where you can schedule a call with us. And what we really do is give you a walkthrough, train you on how to use the dashboard, be able to get you familiar with the methodology behind all our services, and if you want to have your sales staff join the call we can conference with you guys on it.

Now, the other thing is, we have clients that do monthly training sessions with us, and you can ask for that - especially if you've got a large potential to grow. The other thing is if your sales staff need the training to be able to respond to these objections, then you can just do what some of our clients do. what some of our clients do is, right before a pitch, they consult us for 15 to 30 minutes to tell them, okay "so what if they say this, how do we respond to that, and what if they say this, how do I respond to that."

There are about a dozen people waiting on our phones all the time, they're the project managers from our partners. They're there to wait for you to call so that they can help you figure out how to do that close. So, please, call and ask us to train your guys on how to respond to these objections.

Question #6

I'm finding it hard to train my sales staff to have our client's best interests at heart. Any advice?

Answer:

Wow, this one's tough. I would say hire the right salesman. And if I were going to give you a couple of characteristics, what we look for in salespeople, and the ones that create a vested interest in seeing their clients develop is we look for naturally curious people, we never hire people who don't read books.

We check for their levels of empathy; we pay for a $10 test for everyone we screen and hire. And what I look for is an empathy score. And the empathy score, you can easily find this on a standard 16PF psychometric test. But there are providers for psychological exams, and for us what we look for is someone who is genuinely curious, great communication skills, but a high level of empathy.

So, for me, I don't think you can train people to care. You have to hire people who care already or at least ones that sympathize quickly or empathize quickly with people they talk to. And we test for empathy, empirically test for empathy. So my answer to this would be, hire the right people, don't train them to become the right people, it'll be incredibly difficult.

Question #7

There are times when I answer all of my prospect's objections but I am still not able to close the deal. What are we doing wrong?

Answer:

    2-   Are you getting them to laugh?

3- Did they tell you exactly what the business objective was, and does SEO answer that?
4- Did you build a desire? And,
5- Did you secure a commitment?

Are you really answering the prospect's objections? Or maybe you are just affirming it. You have to be careful about that.

Now also, before you disqualify the failure to close because even for us a close on a call is rare. It's rare, we have prospects that close with us after 287 days. So, our sunsetting policy for a lead is tremendously long. SEO is still very much unknown territory; it's a 20-year-old industry, but a lot of people still don't know it that well.

So, don't disqualify your lead very quickly, but if you're not able to close the deal, what I would say is-

A} you might be talking more than they are,
B} you didn't get them to talk enough,
C} you didn't get them to laugh, and I think that's what you would be doing wrong.

Question #8

If a prospect asked me if I was working with their competitor - and I was - what do I do? How do I respond?

Answer:

So, here's what I would say to the partner. I would be very careful. Yes, we do work with your client's competitors, but we do make sure that the campaign is assigned to a different project manager, that way there isn't any conflict of interest. And 9 times out of 10 there would be a difference in the strategy and the budget of a client.

They may be doing a different approach, the other one is probably doing a more holistic marketing approach, they're not just doing SEO, and they're also doing PPC or social media. So, those are the things that we can take into consideration.

Now this one is a matter of personal ethics. I don't necessarily advise that you take the same approach that we do, but you have to understand that I think finding a good, effective, morally imperative partner is incredibly difficult. And I feel that I'm not doing the right thing if I don't do my best to try to close someone because in my opinion their interest will best be served with me.

So, when I get asked this, do you guys work with my competitor, I tell them I don't have an exclusivity policy but I do have a Don't Ask, Don't Tell policy. So, if they ask, I will tell them. But I tell them I don't offer exclusivity; I'll work with anyone that needs competent service because it's fair; it's a free market. And I think that I'm really good at what I do. But see, I've got a Don't Ask, Don't Tell policy. If they don't ask, I won't tell, and neither of us has to be uncomfortable.

Question #9
My client wants me to do Black Hat SEO tactics to gain fast results, and then move to White Hate. What do I do?"
Answer:
Don't do it. There are a lot of legit SEO activities that you can do to gain fast results. Black Hat SEO mostly has to do with link building, but why don't you focus on On-Page?

The returns of really strong, really focused On-Page activities are seen in two to three weeks, all the way to six weeks down the road, and you benefit from it continuously, by the way. On-Page activities, you reap the benefits from strong On-Page activities every two to three weeks, every time a quality score is updated you get better rankings and better rankings and better rankings.

So, if someone wants you to do Black Hat SEO tactics, go for legit On Page. There are over 200 search metrics that you can leverage to your client's advantage. And Black Hat only leverages Off-Page. So, it's not a very powerful strategy. It's not the most powerful metric - still fairly powerful, but not **THE** most powerful.

Question #10

How can I prove to my client that I'm better than a competitor?"

Answer:

Rank a keyword better than a competitor. That's how I would solve this. For all our clients, we watch the rankings like a hawk, and we make sure that they're number one for a specific keyword. It doesn't matter if it's SEO, SEO company, Search Engine Optimization company... it doesn't matter.

You have to be number one for anyone term that's relevant to you, and then you can prove to the client that you use your services, and this is what you get, and all your leads come from that search term. You don't have to outrank them on every query, you just have to outrank them on one keyword.

Schedule a Call

So, now the ball is in your hands as they say. What's it going to be? Will you get better or stay the same? We have materials to help you with your business and they are for free. Just go to **this page** (https://www.easyimreviews.com/blog/digital-marketing-pdf-free-download/) and find out more and download them all.

So once again go sign up and get your very own **Account Manager** (https://www.easyimreviews.com/blog/seo-reseller-review-best-seo-reseller-program/)

Also, download the Digital Marketing Statistics Infographic **Here** (https://www.easyimreviews.com/blog/seo-reseller-review-best-seo-reseller-program/)

PLEASE HELP ME BY LEAVING A REVIEW | HERE ARE THE DIFFERENT REGIONS

US - https://www.amazon.com/dp/B07ZC45CQY

UK - https://www.amazon.co.uk/dp/B07ZC45CQY
CA - https://www.amazon.ca/dp/B07ZC45CQY
AU - https://www.amazon.com.au/dp/B07ZC45CQY
IN - https://www.amazon.in/dp/B07ZC45CQY

www.ingramcontent.com/pod-product-compliance
Lightning Source LLC
Chambersburg PA
CBHW070900220526
45466CB00005B/2065